"Candid, impactful, and nuanced—while also rea.... you want to reduce stress, feel grounded in the midst of turmoil, and ṣₜₒₚ letting the unimportant and inconsequential drive your life, these practices are for you. Stemming from the authors' decades-long practice and experience, they invite you to rest in the richness of the present moment and let its wisdom guide you along."

> —**Riitta H. Rutanen Whaley, MS, MSPH, RYT,**
> mindfulness-based stress reduction (MBSR) and yoga instructor
> at Duke Health and Well-Being, and author of *Pausing Mindfully*

"Jeffrey Brantley and Wendy Millstine brilliantly bring the practice of mindfulness into practical, easily digestible, yet deeply meaningful five-minute sessions. These brief sessions teach us how to be with ourselves in a completely different way—with a sense of friendliness toward self. Brantley's wisdom, warmth of heart, and genuine kindness shine through each of these simple yet powerful practices, and show us how being in the moment with nonjudgmental awareness can transform our lives."

> —**Lisa Wickham,** registered nurse, certified mindfulness
> instructor, certified hypnotherapist, certified compassion
> fatigue practitioner, and owner of Fully Mindful

"This book is a must! In this fast-paced world, *Five Good Minutes of Mindfulness* offers short meditation practices to create some calm and space in our daily lives. Brantley and Millstine have put together a practical and easy approach for creating a habit of self-care, awareness, and wellness."

> —**Betsy Dessauer, MFA, CYT, CWMF,** founder and
> CEO of Mindful Anytime

"What a delight to see another *Five Good Minutes*® book from Brantley and Millstine! In today's busy world, these mini practices make mindfulness accessible to all. Readers will discover one hundred creative ways to access their own resourcefulness, bringing the best version of themselves to meet the challenges of work and life."

—Julie Kosey, MS, PCC, NBC-HWC, CMT-P, RYT,
    director of human performance coaching at Adventist Health,
    MBSR instructor at Duke Integrative Medicine, and faculty
    for UCLA's Training in Mindfulness Facilitation

"What a deal! Five minutes of reflection and practice for a day of greater clarity, focus, peace, and fulfillment. Brantley and Millstine have written a book made for these times. The practices in this book increase awareness and commitment to personal intention while providing a guidepost for staying true to them. This book is a sure medium for staying grounded and empowered, regardless of whether or not the world cooperates."

—Paul Nagy, LCMHC, LCAS, assistant professor in the
    department of psychiatry and behavioral sciences at Duke
    University School of Medicine

"We all have the natural ability to be mindful. And, we all have five minutes! In their latest book filled with easy, accessible self-help practices, Jeff Brantley and Wendy Millstine skillfully guide us in slowing, relaxing, appreciating, and connecting through mindfulness. For anyone looking to boost their inner resilience during these difficult times, *Five Good Minutes of Mindfulness* is a gem."

—Jeff Greeson, PhD, assistant professor of psychology, and director of
    the Mindfulness, Stress and Health Lab at Rowan University

5 GOOD MINUTES of MINDFULNESS

Reduce Stress, Reset, *and* Find Peace Right Now

JEFFREY BRANTLEY, MD
WENDY MILLSTINE

New Harbinger Publication, Inc.

Publisher's Note

This publication is designed to provide accurate and authoritative information in regard to the subject matter covered. It is sold with the understanding that the publisher is not engaged in rendering psychological, financial, legal, or other professional services. If expert assistance or counseling is needed, the services of a competent professional should be sought.

Library of Congress Cataloging-in-Publication Data

Names: Brantley, Jeffrey, author. | Millstine, Wendy, 1966- author.
Title: Five good minutes of mindfulness : reduce stress, reset, and find peace right now / Jeffrey Brantley, MD, and Wendy Millstine, NC.
Other titles: 5 good minutes of mindfulness
Description: Oakland, CA : New Harbinger Publications, Inc., [2022]
Identifiers: LCCN 2021031368 | ISBN 9781684038664 (trade paperback)
Subjects: LCSH: Mindfulness (Psychology) | Self-actualization (Psychology) | Contentment.
Classification: LCC BF637.M56 B74 2022 | DDC 158.1/3--dc23
LC record available at https://lccn.loc.gov/2021031368

Printed in the United States of America

23   22   21

10   9   8   7   6   5   4   3   2   1   First Printing

I wish to dedicate this book to the frontline workers and first responders who have given so much that we could all make it through the time of the COVID-19 pandemic. May these practices support you and be a reminder of the boundless wisdom and goodness that are always there for you within.

—Jeffrey Brantley

In loving memory and in honor of my Uncle Donald David Stone (1942–2021).

—Wendy Millstine

CONTENTS

PART 2: APPRECIATING WHO YOU ARE AND WHAT YOU HAVE

PART 3: CONNECTING TO OTHERS AND THE WORLD AROUND YOU

PREFACE

The world has changed a great deal since the first Five Good Minutes book was published in 2005. Unfortunately, those changes have been for the worse in many cases. Present-day challenges and threats from environmental warming, persistent global violence, the politicization and weaponization of personal values, widespread abuses by emboldened authoritarian governments, and deeply embedded racist ideologies and institutions are now relentlessly pressing into our collective consciousness on a daily basis. These times most certainly call for responses that are well informed and courageous, if we wish to survive and to save and promote life on our planet.

Choosing wise, prosocial, and effective action is difficult in any circumstance, but the challenges of these times, especially, can hit home in very personal ways for each of us and interfere with our responses to situations in our day-to-day lives. For instance, nationwide studies reveal increased anxiety, fear, and grief in large numbers among those surveyed. Stress in daily life is greater for many reasons, including loss of income, isolation, and mandates to work from home and to home-school as well as restrictions on movement, recreation, and contact with distant loved ones as a result of crises like the COVID-19 pandemic.

The good news, however, is that something very valuable, powerful, and positive has NOT changed since 2005. That is the possibility and ability each of us has to tap into enormous inner resources that include mindfulness, kindness, joy, compassion, and wise understanding.

Mindfulness is simply the dimension in each of us that knows what is happening while it is happening. It is the part that knows what is happening now—as when awareness recognizes that the mind is busy thinking, or when the touch of a breeze feels cool to the skin, or when the upset of anxiety and fear is a felt presence in mind and body. Mindfulness is the part of us that simply knows and is aware of the experience present for us in this moment. And we each already have all the mindfulness we need. We don't have to do anything special to create it or change ourselves in any way to get "more" or "enough" mindfulness. We only need to recognize, trust, and make our home more steadily in this dimension of knowing that is always present within us, within our wholeness as human beings.

The practices in this book offer easy-to-follow methods to establish mindfulness and to inhabit each moment or activity you do mindfully. They encourage you to explore and rest in that dimension of noticing and knowing, which also means relaxing and resting in present-moment awareness and simply letting things be the way they are—and then learning and acting wisely from what you notice.

It may seem odd to simply let things be the way they are, especially when life is painful. But from an awareness of the present-moment—with mindfulness—one can more easily access and intentionally explore the basic human qualities of kindness, compassion, joy, and steadfast presence. Being mindfully present can also support investigation, discovery, and even gratitude for the experience of being embodied—the experience of living your life within this miraculous human body.

Some of the practices in this book will encourage you to begin mindfully and then intentionally investigate other qualities and experiences. As you do this, you not only will discover more about yourself but also perhaps find a place of refuge in well-being that you were not aware of. This knowledge and awareness will support you as you face challenges and make decisions, whatever they may be, in your daily life.

When our every moment is informed by mindfulness and when we are more in touch with our good-heartedness and other positive qualities that are linked to our deepest values and experience as human beings, we become increasingly likely to make the wisest and most effective choices for action in any moment. Whether we are dealing with a loved one's upset or some danger that threatens a dear one, whether we are acknowledging our own pain or distress or the call for action within the larger community or even throughout the world, tapping into our inner resources of awareness, good-heartedness, and wisdom can provide a trustworthy compass to guide us forward.

I know I speak for my colleague and coauthor, Wendy Millstine, as well as for all the folks at New Harbinger Publications in wishing you many experiences of peace, ease, wisdom, joy, and a growing trust in yourself and your own possibilities as you explore these practices. They will help you learn to slow down and relax, appreciate what you have, and connect with others and the world around you. We encourage you to recall—at all times—that you already have what you need of these qualities. These practices are simply allies and guides that will help you connect with, remember, trust, and manifest your deepest wisdom.

—Jeffrey Brantley, MD
Durham, NC

THE FOUNDATION:

WHAT ARE FIVE GOOD MINUTES?

Five minutes is clock time. The practices and activities in this book invite you to dwell in the present moment—which is both always here and always timeless.

We believe that five minutes of clock time transforms your experience into something much more powerful and interesting when you are fully present in this moment (and not lost in thoughts of past or future), when you set a clear intention for your actions, and when you act wholeheartedly. The exercises in this book aim to cultivate peace and relaxation, deepen awareness and connection to life, enhance relationships, and develop kindness and wisdom, so when you apply attention, intention, and wholeheartedness to them, your five minutes truly become five *good* minutes.

WHY FIVE MINUTES IN THE MORNING?

While you can do these practices at any time of day, and although some practices are meant to be used in specific contexts (such as during your workday or before going to bed), we suggest doing them first thing in the morning—especially if you're just beginning a practice of mindfulness. For many of us, the morning is the best time to break away from old habits of thinking and feeling and to set a new direction for ourselves, including how we will be in our day.

How do you usually begin your day now? Do the same thoughts, feelings, and worries fill your head when you open your eyes in the morning? Do you handle them in the same ways? Does one day begin to feel just like the previous one?

We all fall into habits of thinking, feeling, and acting. We seek distraction and relief and something better in our lives. Too often, however, we don't know where to start. Yet so much of what we seek is actually within us. The exercises in this book invite you to take five good minutes and begin to discover what lies within you. They invite you to be more playful, to experiment and become more curious about your life. They offer a way to awaken yourself, instead of being on "automatic pilot," so you can discover something different about yourself and about life. Ultimately, the combination of attention, intention, and wholeheartedness offers you a radically different way of approaching life. Any exercise in this book—done in the morning—has the power to impact greatly on your experience throughout the day, if you allow it to do so!

LEARNING BY DOING

As you experiment and practice with the hundred exercises in this book, you will learn to consciously apply your attention, intention, and wholeheartedness to life. You will see for yourself the power of being present and acting with intention while doing guided exercises. And you may even discover more ways beyond the hundred exercises to apply these same principles throughout your life.

To begin, all you need is some curiosity and the willingness to take the practices in this book seriously enough to try them.

You will learn to establish presence—an accepting and allowing awareness—by practicing mindful and kind attention to the simple sensations of your breath. Being present in this way is the doorway to the timeless now. Mindful attention to the breath is not the only way to be more present, but it is a good way, and you always have your breath with you! Paying attention to the breath in a way that does not try to change, add, or subtract anything to the present moment has been practiced by human beings for thousands of years as a way to enter and remain here now.

With your presence established and dwelling more consciously in the present moment, you can set your intention for the activity or practice you have chosen.

Intention is potent. Nothing you do in this human life happens without some preexisting intention. Think of it. No movement or action happens without some thought, idea, or intent beforehand. Many movements occur from intentions that are unconscious or semiconscious, but if you pay close enough attention, you will observe the decision to act (or react, if the decision is unconscious) before you act.

In your five good minutes, therefore, the second step is to set your intention. It might be "May this meditation support peace and ease in my life." Or it could be "May this activity awaken humor and joy in me."

The remaining three to five minutes of your five good minutes are devoted to a specific exercise or activity. This book takes more than one approach to mindfulness. You don't have to like or even try all the exercises. Feel free to work with the ones that speak to you. But you might also benefit from experimenting with exercises that do not initially appeal to you. Try to explore!

To review, here are the three easy steps to your five good minutes:

1. Establish presence through mindful breathing.

2. Set your intention.

3. Do the exercise or activity you have chosen wholeheartedly—in a way in which you are mindful, fully present, and completely connected to what you are doing.

Many exercises in this book will invite you to breathe mindfully and to set your intention before moving on to the remaining instructions. Others will not refer directly to attention and intention before giving the exercise instructions. Even if it is not suggested directly, it would be a good idea to take a few mindful breaths and to set an intention before you begin an exercise.

To appreciate the power of attention and intention, you might even experiment by doing the same exercise without establishing attention and intention, and then repeat it with them. See for yourself how powerful being present and setting intention really are for the experience of five good minutes.

EXERCISES AND ACTIVITIES

You will work with a variety of approaches in your five good minutes. They include the following:

Mindfulness is the awareness that arises as you pay attention on purpose, with a friendly and accepting attitude to whatever is present. Being mindful means consciously being present. Being mindful is at the heart of your five good minutes. Mindfulness of your breath is how you establish presence. The exercises in this book aim to help you become more mindful in different places and in different ways in your daily life.

Meditation is an activity of directing your attention so that you will become more aware, more understanding, and wiser. Meditation is about much more than simple relaxation. Some meditation methods emphasize narrowing your attention to a single object or a quality so you can learn to sharpen and train your awareness. Other meditation practices focus upon developing a clearer and deeper awareness of what is actually happening. The meditation practices in this book include both approaches. They promote calm attention and awareness for feeling more ease and peace, for greater understanding, and for the development of desirable qualities, such as kindness, compassion, and joy.

Imagery is the thought process that involves and uses the senses: vision, audition, smell, taste, and the senses of movement and position. You use your imagination to facilitate communication between perception, emotion, and bodily change. It is one of the world's oldest healing resources.

Finally, *acting wholeheartedly* is central to all the activities. Many offer suggestions for doing everyday things just a little differently—being more present and mindful, connecting more completely with what you do in the present moment, then singing, laughing, dancing, eating, listening—in short, participating in a whole array of experiences wholeheartedly. See for yourself the difference that being present can make!

WHAT HAPPENS NEXT?

When you do your five good minutes, it is important to expect nothing more. Just be as present as possible in the five minutes and pay attention throughout the rest of the day. Notice how the exercise you do at the start of a day can echo and inform your experience throughout the day.

Doing just one of these exercises with presence and intention has the power to change how you feel and relate to your life. Yet don't be discouraged if it seems nothing is different. You can also think of the five good minutes as planting a seed. It can take some time for a seed to grow. Again, a good idea is to just do the practice and to expect nothing while remaining open to everything. You never know when one of these practices will be a doorway for you, or a new beginning, or even a lifeline. Just keep alert to what does happen.

Of course, you can experiment with more than five minutes in any of the exercises. And you can do your five good minutes more than once each day, or at some time other than the morning (though, again, morning is often best).

You can carry your favorite five good minutes' practices further and go deeper by doing them more often, by reading and learning more about any subject that the practice suggests, and by associating with others who enjoy similar activities.

In other words, your five good minutes in the morning might just change your life.

YOUR GATEWAY TO THE PRESENT MOMENT

"Breathe mindfully for about a minute."

You will see this phrase at the beginning of many of the exercises in this book.

Why?

To be mindful means to connect with experience unfolding in the present moment—by paying deep and nonjudging attention. Practicing mindfulness promotes presence, the capacity to sense the immediacy of experience in each moment.

Any action you do—indeed, your involvement in any activity (including your five good minutes)—is enormously amplified by the extent you are present with awareness.

Despite a desire to be more present for life, however, everyone has habits of inattention, distraction, and absence. These habits separate you from the richness in life's moments and from people with whom you wish a closer and more lasting connection.

Learning to practice mindful breathing, as you will in this book, can help you overcome habits of inattention and be more present for yourself and for life. Mindful breathing (also known as awareness of breathing or mindfulness of breathing) is one of the most ancient and profound meditation practices available to human beings. It can be done by anyone, regardless of faith. Whoever you are, paying attention on purpose and nonjudgmentally to the sensations of your breath is an effective way to dwell in the present moment and to avoid being lost in the wanderings of your own mind.

To breathe mindfully means to become a kind observer of your own breath sensations as they move in and out of your body. As you become an increasingly sensitive observer, you will begin to notice different qualities in each breath, in or out, and the space between the breaths. And by practicing even one minute of mindful breathing before setting an intention and doing the rest of your five good minutes, you will establish yourself more fully in the present moment. This will add more power to the exercise you are doing.

In addition to doing the meditation practices in this book, you may want to explore longer periods of meditation with mindful breathing, using the instructions below.

INSTRUCTIONS FOR MINDFUL BREATHING

The following instructions are one way to practice mindful breathing. Some of the exercises in this book will elaborate further on mindful breathing. You may also be aware of other variations on these instructions. Whatever the exact wording may be, mindful breathing is essentially about your willingness to reside in the present moment with your kind and nonjudging attention focused primarily on the sensations of your breath. From that primary focus, your relationship to all other experience shifts.

Please remember also that you can do mindful breathing in any position—sitting, lying down, or standing—and even while moving.

Now, let these instructions guide you as you practice mindful breathing here and later in this book:

Take a comfortable position, one that supports you in being awake.

Turn your attention on purpose to the physical sensations happening as you breathe. You may wish to close your eyes if it helps you focus attention on your breath sensations.

Find a place in your body—the tip of your nose or your abdomen, for example—where you can actually feel the breath moving in and out.

Rest your attention there, where you can feel your breath most easily.

It is not necessary to control your breath in any way in this meditation. Simply allow your body to breathe as it does, and pay attention as best you can to the direct sensations of the moving breath.

As you direct kind attention to your breath sensations, set down all of your burdens—inner and outer ones—for the time of this meditation. It is not necessary to make anything happen nor to become anything other than who you are in this moment.

When you notice that your attention has wandered off the breath sensations, notice where it went, and then gently but firmly bring your attention back. You have not done anything wrong when this happens. The mind will move off the breath countless times. Each time, practice kindness and patience with yourself, notice where your mind went, and bring attention back to the breath.

Let the meditation support you. Rest attention on the changing patterns of sensation and breath. Move your attention closer, noticing the quality of each new breath as accurately and as continuously as possible. Stay present to the entire breath cycle: in, pause, out, pause, in, and so on. Notice how each breath has its own character.

End your meditation by shifting your focus off the breath sensations, opening your eyes, and moving gently, bringing your awareness from your breath back into the rest of your body.

SET YOUR INTENTION

Setting an intention is a way of pointing yourself in a direction, toward an important value or goal. It is a way to identify a quality you wish to nurture in your life so that your practice becomes all about nurturing that quality.

Setting intention can be done skillfully, in a way that aids your practice, or unskillfully, in a way that undermines it.

It is not so skillful or effective to be rigid or attached to an ideal about your intention. For example, if your intention is to foster ease and self-acceptance, don't expect to become 100 percent relaxed or self-accepting after just five minutes! And be careful that you don't make your intention, no matter how wonderful or positive, something else on your to-do list or something you must achieve at all costs. Recognize the trap of judging yourself harshly or doubting your intention if things don't change right away. Don't fall into that trap of judgment and doubt. It harms your practice more than it helps.

A skillful intention is more like a friendly guide. Acknowledge from the beginning that important changes take time. You, like everyone else, must make the effort to return repeatedly to the goal you seek.

Your intention, to become more self-accepting, for example, is better thought of as a direction you have selected for yourself. The practice you choose is a way of following a path moving in that direction. Many conditions and factors are at work as you move along your path. And results aren't always so obvious. What is important is that you keep moving in the right direction. Being friendly with yourself as you travel the path is vital. Being patient with yourself as you move toward your goal is crucial.

You can think of your intention as a clear and strong statement of an important value, quality, or goal you have selected for yourself. Through the single act of making the statement, you have opened the door for a profound shift in your life.

ACT WHOLEHEARTEDLY

To act wholeheartedly means to do something with all of your attention and energy. In your five good minutes, after establishing presence and stating an intention, you are invited to embrace the practice you have selected wholeheartedly. Establishing presence and acting from clear intention will support you in embracing what you do wholeheartedly.

You may have to experiment a bit with being wholehearted. Much of what we do in life is done without full attention or without real commitment to the activity or process, for a variety of reasons. So, as you begin the exercises in this book, give yourself some room to grow. At first, you may not feel wholehearted about every one of the exercises. Some may even be a turnoff.

To get the most of your five good minutes, start with activities that resonate with you, or that seem especially interesting, or that are perfect for something happening in your life right now. As you work with the various practices over time, notice how different ones fit in the different corners and phases of your life.

When you have selected practices that seem to fit, nurture a willingness to experiment with them, without expecting too much at first. Even if you feel awkward, silly, or embarrassed, just acknowledge how you feel and then keep on with the practice.

You may find it easier to be wholehearted if you let go of trying to change anything or make anything happen as you do the exercises. This is a paradox that is true of many of the practices in this book. In the realm of transformation and growth, the more you reach for something, the farther away it can seem.

So, let go of any attachment to outcome and just dive right in! Instead of vigilantly monitoring what is happening, looking for changes when dancing, or laughing, or whatever you are practicing, just let go of judgment and do it—do the practice. That way, you are truly acting wholeheartedly and, paradoxically, you maximize your chances for change and growth.

PART 1

SLOWING DOWN
AND RELAXING

The concept is simple: take the time, just five minutes every day, to be present, to set a clear intention for yourself, and to allow yourself to relax. As with any new endeavor, it's wise to start out slowly—and with these exercises, slowing down is the name of the game. We'll cover basic skills first (breathing, body scanning, self-hypnosis), later turning to exercises that will help you apply those skills in specific contexts, like the workplace or before bed. Let's dive in.

1 BREATHE MINDFULLY

Worries, busyness, pain, and upset are real. They happen to you and can create feelings of isolation and disconnection.

It is important and helpful to recognize when such separation happens and also to recognize that, although these intense energies are yours, they are not *you!*

Mindful breathing can help you realize and remember that you are more than any challenging energy. It can allow you to rest in a steadier and wider dimension.

- Select a time and place where you will not be disturbed.

- Breathe mindfully for about a minute.

- Set your intention. For example, "May mindful breathing bring me peace and wisdom."

- For the rest of this practice, relax and just breathe mindfully.

- Remember that mindful breathing is not a breathing exercise. It is an awareness practice.

- Let sensitivity, kindness, and awareness grow in you as you repeatedly let the breath sensations "back in."

2 RELAX DEEPLY

How often do you wish you could calm down or just relax?

Everyone has a built-in capacity for deep relaxation, but they may not appreciate or know how to access it. This practice will teach you a way to connect with your own ability for deep inner relaxation.

- Breathe mindfully for about a minute.

- Set your intention. For example, "May this practice of deep relaxation bring me health and ease."

- Focus mindfully on the sensations of your breath, in and out.

- Imagine that you are inhaling calm and peace. With each out-breath, exhale any unnecessary tension in your body.

- Breathe this way for a few more minutes. Let the actual flow of your breath support you, bringing in peace and carrying out tension.

- End by opening your eyes and moving gently.

3 WISH YOURSELF SAFETY

The feeling of safety is priceless and often elusive. Even the possibility of safety may at times seem unreachable.

There is profound power in the simple gesture of wishing safety for yourself. As a meditation, this practice is done in the same spirit of a parent holding a frightened child and lovingly whispering soothing words.

- Breathe mindfully for about a minute.

- Set your intention. For example, "May this practice support a deeper peace and ease in me."

- Relax, let your eyes close, and imagine a picture of yourself.

- Bring compassionate attention to yourself, as a parent would to a child.

- For the next few minutes, imagine speaking directly to yourself, whispering a phrase like "May I be safe from all harm" or "May I be protected from all inner and outer harm." Wish yourself safety with the same spirit you would wish a dear friend a safe trip.

- End by opening your eyes and moving gently.

4 LIVE IN THIS MOMENT

Life is happening in this moment, yet how much of your attention is directed to planning for the future or trying to undo or correct the past (even when you don't need or want to be planning or correcting)?

This practice helps you become more aware of the habit of the mind to move out of the present moment. Recognizing habits of inattention and absence will empower you to become free and to live more fully in the present.

- Breathe mindfully for about a minute.

- Set your intention. For example, "May this practice free me from habits of absence and inattention."

- For the next few minutes, notice any thoughts you have directed at either the future or the past. Acknowledge them and say thank you. You don't have to fight with them. Just let them go.

- If you become distracted or confused, breathe mindfully for a few breaths. When you are focused again, return your attention to the thoughts. Learn to recognize when your attention goes to the future or to the past.

- End by opening your eyes and moving gently.

5 FIVE-FINGERED PEACE

With a little practice, in just five minutes you can induce a highly effective relaxation technique using just your hand. Follow the steps below to guide yourself to a centered, focused state of awareness.

- Touching your thumb to your index finger, travel back to a time when you felt a healthy exhaustion after exerting yourself physically, such as cleaning house, mowing the lawn, or biking.

- Touching your thumb to your middle finger, travel back in time to a loving exchange with someone special, such as a devoted love letter, a tantalizing sexual experience, or a heart-expanding conversation.

- Touching your thumb to your ring finger, try to recollect the most caring gesture you have ever received. Take this opportunity to truly accept this gift.

- Touching your thumb to your little finger, travel back to the most magnificent place that you've seen or dreamed about. Take this moment to absorb all the beauty that surrounds you.

This five-finger relaxation is your ticket to building inner strength, harmony, and a sense of ease.

6 IN WITH THE GOOD...

When you take the time to get in tune with your breathing, you begin to harness the vital life skills for returning to your calm, inner self. Sitting or lying down, place your hand on your abdomen and inhale and exhale, deeply and slowly. Visualize a meadow with a small creek running through it. You are wading in a babbling brook, and you can hear the wind and the birds overhead. The current tugs gently at your ankles. Recognize the rhythm of your breathing. As you inhale, say the word "warm" aloud. Imagine the warmth of the sun and water around your body. As you exhale, say the word "heavy" to yourself. Allow yourself to reach a comfortable and soothing place from within. Conscious breathing is a technique that can restore calmness to your day easily, in less than five minutes.

7 INSTANT AHHHH...

When you are triggered by stress and anger, you need a way to induce relaxation instantly. You need a cue, like the command "Relax," in order to reduce your anxiety as quickly as possible. Get comfortable in a seated position. Take a deep breath and hold it for an extra moment. When you release this breath, focus on blowing your worries far away. Let go of any excess tension still residing in your body. Continue to breathe in and out, deeply and rhythmically, saying to yourself silently, "Breathe in" on the inhale and "Relax" on the exhale. Follow this repetition for five minutes:

Breathe in...

Breathe out... Relax...

Breathe in...

Breathe out... Relax...

Breathe in...

Breathe out... Relax...

With each breath, peace and calm come in, and tension and stress move out.

8 A SILENT RETREAT

Take five minutes to quiet your mind. Turn off the radio. Ask the kids or your partner or whoever you live with to give you a few precious moments without a sound. In the silence, you can notice your breathing, your anxiety, your urgency. In the silence, you can stretch your mind to a place of calm, less stress, with no rush to be anywhere but right where you are. A moment in silence can set the tone for the rest of your busy day. With your eyes open or closed, the calming powers of silence can carry you through any stressful situation. Keep this center of calmness and stillness with you wherever you go. The restorative power of silent solitude can be used to give you a sense of ease.

9 FREEDOM FROM TENSION

Our bodies are a breeding ground for tension. We might store up tension for weeks before we know it's there. Headaches, backaches, and other physical pains are the voices of our bodies crying out for attention. Acknowledge and release your tension using a body scan technique.

- Lying down, take five minutes to scan where tension lives in your body.

- Start at the top of your head and move along down your neck, back, arms, and legs, noting the areas where you store your stress.

- Once you have identified those areas, follow a simple guided imagery of becoming a free-floating cloud. High above the skyline, you are impervious to all negative thoughts and tension. In your free-floating bliss, all muscles and pains are released and set free.

Carry this imagery with you and use it whenever you need a sense of tranquility.

10 BE A MOUNTAIN

This is a good practice for those times when you feel scattered, off balance, or unfocused.

It allows you to reconnect with the elemental quality of earthiness and strength within. Doing this practice can ground you deeply in the present moment.

- Stand or sit comfortably.

- Breathe mindfully for about a minute.

- Set your intention. For example, "May this practice help me find inner strength."

- Imagine the most beautiful mountain you have ever seen, either in person or in a photograph.

- As you visualize your mountain, let your body become the mountain. Feel the same qualities of steadiness, strength, unshakeableness, and majesty.

- For the next few minutes, rest in your "mountain body," unmoved by any thoughts, fears, worries, or other experiences around you, just as the mountain is unmoved by any weather patterns around it.

- End by opening your eyes and moving gently.

11 RELEASE THE TRAP

When stressful thoughts inundate us, we all need a quick-fix coping technique. Coping mantras are a simple way to redirect your focus away from anxious thoughts. Positive coping statements enable you to talk yourself through any stressful occurrence. Here are some possible affirmations that will help guide you in your efforts to remain calm and focused. Speak these words aloud:

"My anxiety will soon pass."

"I am okay. I am safe. I can cope with any stress that comes my way."

"I have support and love from others around me."

"I trust my ability to handle this stress in a calm way."

"I am choosing to relax now because there will be time later to take action."

Carry these strengthening and calming coping declarations with you throughout your day. By giving yourself permission to find your calm, centered place, you move away from the trapped feelings of anxiety and put yourself in a more pleasant frame of mind.

12 SOFT BELLY

You can be surrounded by all the love you could ever want, but when your life gets maxed out with stress, frustration, and fatigue, love may not be enough. Take this five-minute mindful reprieve to slow down your pace and relax into the moment.

- Begin seated in a quiet and comfortable space, if possible.

- Close your eyes and take a few slow breaths, acknowledging and then letting go of any pockets of tension with each exhale.

- Now focus on softening your belly, releasing any tightened muscles or feelings of anxiety. Let your belly go limp, allowing it to rise and fall with each breath.

- Worries and stresses may wander in and out of your mind, but keep your attention on your relaxed belly.

When love falls short of your expectations, just remember that a soft belly helps maintain a relaxed mind. And when you're feeling calm, love and happiness can find their way back into your life.

13 THE DOCTOR IS IN

Each of us has the ability to be a healer. It is an ancient wisdom and gift deeply ingrained in our species, but rarely do we give ourselves the permission to cultivate our healing nature. Take a few minutes and scan your mind and body for areas of pain or discomfort, physical or emotional. Become your own shaman. Ask your higher self what you need to help assist you in healing your aches and pains.

- Do you need more rest?

- Do you need more water?

- How does your body feel and what can you do for yourself to feel better?

- Would a cup of herbal tea help you to relax right now?

Cultivate your inner healer and imagine that you have the insight and power to meet all of your health needs.

14 DROP IT

Self-hypnosis is a simple skill that allows you to quickly reach a peaceful place. Find a pencil, and hold it so that it dangles a few inches above a table. Let your eyes gently focus on the tip of the pencil. When you've reached a deeply relaxed state of mind, the pencil will drop. The sound of the pencil hitting the table will alert you to summon a healing, five-minute meditative trance. Begin your self-hypnosis by saying to yourself, "I am drifting off into a deep, deep, tranquil space…I am beginning to feel sleepy and drowsy, drowsy and sleepy…My eyes are heavy and my body is relaxed and letting go…I am free of all unnecessary thoughts and feelings…I am floating, drifting, drifting and floating, into a place of total relaxation." If your pencil has not dropped by this time, release it now, and enjoy the next few minutes of a serene hypnosis.

15 DRAIN THE STRAIN

Few of us think of our work space as a refuge for meditation. But even in the sometimes hectic realm of work, you can find inner and outer space for peace. The next exercise can be done at your desk, the office hallway, or even outside.

- In a standing position, inhale slowly and deeply from the diaphragm. Exhale, and let your jaw, tongue, arms, and shoulders go completely loose. Feel the heaviness throughout your entire body, pulsating down your arms and legs as though they were hollow drainpipes.

- With each inhale, imagine gusts of refreshing air flushing the tension through these pipes and pushing it out at your fingertips and toes with each exhale.

- Shake out your body thoroughly by jiggling your shoulders to each side and swinging your arms to and fro. You can also jiggle each leg, one at a time.

When you recognize your stress levels maxing out, take five minutes to decompress, unwind, and shake out your mounting tension.

16 WATCH YOUR SPEED

Hurry and momentum from the workday is easily internalized and, like a rapid drumbeat, can dictate your inner tempo long after your workday ends. Near the end of your workday, experiment with shifting to a different tempo.

- Find a place that offers privacy.

- Breathe or listen mindfully for about a minute.

- Set your intention. For example, "May this practice bring me ease and joy."

- Bring attention to your mind and body. Are your thoughts racing? Is there tension anywhere in your body? Is either your mind or your body agitated?

- Stand up and start consciously moving your body at a speed that matches your inner speed. Walk, shake, or move for about a minute, really feeling the sensations.

- Now take another minute or two and slow down deliberately, gently, and consciously, until you are stopped. Sit down.

- Relax and breathe mindfully.

- End by moving out at your new speed.

17 A MATTER OF HEART

There's nothing more uncomfortable than starting your work morning with a stressor from your personal life clawing at your mind. The following practice will restore inner balance and calm, which will initiate the process of healing whatever ails the heart.

- Begin by placing your hand over your heart with the purpose of locating your heartbeat.

- Once you've found your heart rhythm, breathe slowly and mindfully into your abdomen. Notice how your breathing can affect your heart rate. Under stress, we tend to take shallow breaths, not filling our lungs and body adequately with oxygen.

- Now breathe more deeply and abundantly, filling your chest cavity with air. How has your heart rhythm changed or relaxed?

- During times of strain in your personal life strain, you may build up physical and emotional tension in your heart. By reconnecting with your heartbeat, you can release excess tension and restore a feeling of centeredness.

18 RESTORE YOUR NATURAL RHYTHM

Under extreme stress, you may tend to hold your breath. Escalating work demands or other forms of stress can cause a shortness of breath. Relentlessly pressing deadlines may push you to the edge of your seat with anxiety, which further obstructs your natural breathing rhythm. The following exercise will assist you in replacing your rocket-fuel stress with peace and serenity.

- Notice the occasions in your workday when tension rises and when your chest may tighten. Notice when your breathing becomes irregular or when you're holding your breath.

- During these times of stress, practice moving more breath into and out of the body, helping your body take in more oxygen. Three long, deep breaths into your belly will work.

- Let go of the belly breathing and allow your body to breathe naturally and at its own depth and rhythm, until you begin to feel a sense of calm rising.

- Pay attention to sensations occurring from the body's natural breathing patterns. Are you feeling less anxious? Are you experiencing a loosening and relaxing in your body?

19 FLOAT AWAY

Stress and workday pressures can make your heart, mind, and body feel increasingly solid and heavy. When you feel this way, what would it be like to soften and open to spaciousness?

- Breathe or listen mindfully for about a minute.

- Set your intention. For example, "May this practice give me ease and lightness."

- Bring your attention to the sensations inside your body. Acknowledge any sense of contraction, holding, or tension.

- Breathe or listen mindfully.

- Shift your attention to your thoughts and feelings. Acknowledge any worry, anxiety, or repeating thoughts.

- Breathe or listen mindfully.

- Imagine that your solid body softens, and that your heart, mind, and body flow together and expand into a beautiful balloon.

- Let the balloon float up and away—as far and as high as feels safe.

- Rest in spaciousness, ease, and lightness.

- End by returning to the ground, now more relaxed.

20 RITUAL FOR RELEASE

Acknowledge where there is tension in your body or your mind. Now take five minutes for the following exercise where you envision the release of all tension throughout your mind, body, and soul.

- Stand with your legs shoulder-width apart and solidly planted on the ground. Your arms should be loose at your sides, and your body should feel relaxed but balanced and strong.

- Now lean forward from your hips and let your upper body hang down toward the ground, with your arms loose and fingertips dangling toward the floor.

- Breathe deeply and relax your body incrementally so that your fingers come closer and closer to the floor and your hips soften and release your torso.

- Close your eyes and visualize your body being completely relaxed.

- To come up without straining your back, remember to roll up slowly, one vertebra at a time, your head coming up last. Stand upright, relaxed, with your hands at your side.

This is a good exercise for releasing tension.

21 RED LIGHT, BLUE LIGHT

Take the next several minutes to visualize your whole body infused with red and blue lights. The red lights represent tension, and the blue lights represent relaxation. You can adjust the lights from brighter to dimmer, from bigger to smaller.

Observe the areas in your body where the lights are red. Now imagine the red lights are just feathers. Pick them up. See yourself opening a window and tossing out your tensions into the wind. Go ahead and dump them all.

Watch them flutter and move farther and farther away. As they disappear from your sight, they will also disappear from your awareness. Be aware of the sensation of all the blue lights of calmness circulating throughout your body. Relax further by visualizing all the blue lights becoming deeper and darker shades. Soon all your tension will be replaced by tranquility.

22 STOP WATCHING THE CLOCK

Why do the last couple of hours of your work shift appear to go by excruciatingly slowly, as if time were at a standstill? If you find yourself watching the second hand on the clock or looking for your car keys an hour before you've even finished your tasks, try this exercise for distracting your mind from the endless clock-watching game.

- Begin by reconnecting with the rhythm of your breathing: inhale and exhale, inhale and exhale. Are you relaxed? Pay attention to your body. Notice the thoughts running through your mind.

- On your in-breath, say aloud or inwardly, "In this breath, I am drawing myself closer to this moment in time."

- On your out-breath, say aloud or inwardly, "In this breath, I am distancing myself from what the future may or may not bring."

- Prioritize the tasks that are in front of you and visualize the satisfaction of crossing off a few more tasks.

Keeping busy and focused on your immediate assignments will maximize your time and give you a sense of accomplishment at the end of your shift.

23 PATIENCE ON THE JOURNEY

If you're accustomed to instant gratification, everything you need at the flick of a switch, your capacity for patience may atrophy like an unused muscle. A sign that impatience has descended is when you start complaining and a feeling of insistence takes over your every thought. You may be thinking to yourself, "I wish she'd hurry up" or "He takes forever to finish his chores." This five-minute meditation will instill a little endurance for just those times:

- Take this moment to stop everything you're doing. Find a place to sit and shut out the world, if possible.

- As you begin to quiet your mind, try to visualize exactly where your patience resides in your body. Perhaps it's on vacation in your mind or has left your body altogether.

- Consider a time when you were not in a hurry, not anxious for your partner to get up to speed, a time when you were simply at ease and serene with the natural flow of life.

- Say your intentions aloud: "I am calling forth the calm winds of patience. May patience always be a lasting and enduring presence in my life."

When you usher in your patience, love and understanding are sure to break through.

24 TAKE A "SHAKE-IT" BREAK

Searing blowups with a loved one can cause a chain reaction of stress and anxiety. Anger has a way of tipping the scales away from the things that you truly value the most in life, such as kindness, empathy, and compromise. A preprogrammed shake-it break can help both of you dissipate the rage. Try it together, if you can.

When tension and anger reach a boiling point, instead of dragging it out indefinitely, negotiate about taking a break, scheduling a time to discuss it later, and then each of you go for a walk or get outside. In the heat of the moment, both of you give yourselves permission to walk away without needing to solve everything immediately. How many arguments ever got resolved during a screaming match?

Once you've walked away with the agreement that you'll work on it later with your partner, find a quiet place to try this physical exercise.

Begin by standing up and shaking out every single part of your body. Come on, don't be self-conscious! Be methodical as you wiggle and jiggle your head, neck, shoulders, arms, wrists, fingers, chest, torso, hips, stomach, legs, ankles, and toes.

- Keep up your movement while you shake out your heavy thoughts and feelings. Imagine all this vibration allowing your anger and hurt to trickle out through your ears.

Don't let anger and resentment destabilize your relationship. Make wiggle room for putting your best foot forward in the direction of resolution.

25 SAFE WITH ME

One of the greatest gifts you can offer another is a feeling of safety in your company. By learning to better manage your own disturbing states of anger and fear, you make your presence safer and more inviting to others. Try this practice for working with your own anger and fear:

- When you notice you are upset or angry, mindfully offer compassion to yourself.

- Breathe, listen, or move mindfully for about a minute.

- Set your intention. For example, "May I manage my own anger and upset wisely."

- Stop fighting the anger or fear. Stop feeding it too. Try making space for it. Feel it in your body. Whatever you feel, breathe mindfully with it.

- Notice any anger- or fear-driven thoughts. Don't fight or feed them. Acknowledge them and let them go. Breathe mindfully with them.

- End by offering yourself an affirmation. For example, "I am stronger and wiser than this upset."

- Move forward.

26 TENSION TAMER

Many jobs require upper-body strength or, at the very least, endurance, whether you work at a computer, in a flower shop, or in a senior facility caring for the elderly. At first, you may experience mild discomfort in your neck and shoulders only to be followed by more intensely crippling pain by the end of the day. Reduce your discomfort dramatically by taking frequent, small breaks to practice an exercise to loosen your neck and shoulders.

- From a standing position or seated at the edge of your chair with your feet shoulder-width apart and leaning your body slightly more forward than your knees, let your arms hang loose at your sides.

- Tilting your head back, raise your eyes to the ceiling, slowly looking as far back as you can and mentally marking the spot on the ceiling. Then gradually bring your chin toward your chest. Be gentle with your neck. Return to a relaxed, upright position.

- Next, draw both shoulders up toward your earlobes, tightening briefly, and then quickly release and drop your arms loosely at your sides.

Repeat this exercise three to five times and observe how much further back your neck can stretch. Your range of motion in your neck and back has likely increased.

27 RELAXING MIND TONIC

After a hectic day of work, errands, and responsibilities, getting a good night's sleep might seem like attempting to stop a fast-moving train on a downhill slope without brakes. Thoughts and tasks to be done tomorrow may be spinning and swirling in your mind with no hope for rest in sight.

Tonight, before you head off to bed, take a couple of minutes to make a cup of calming herbal tea, such as chamomile or peppermint. (Some herbal teas can be stimulating, so choose wisely or seek advice if you're uncertain.) Even if you don't have a taste for the tea, the ritual of preparing it is part of the passage of calming your nerves. During this process, take notice of every detail: What mug did you select? How does the tea smell, even before you brew it? Notice the sound of the kettle filling with water, the feel of its weight in your hand, the hissing of water drops dissipating on the stove, the heat emanating from the kettle, the boiling water splashing into your cup, the tendrils of white steam rising from your tea, and the calming aromatic fragrance.

28 STAR-FILLED NIGHTS

When was the last time you stood outside beneath the stars? Even if you live in a city where you can't see them or at times when fog or clouds block your view, you know with absolute certainty that you're standing under the magnificent array of stars that stretch across the universe.

Let yourself spend a few minutes stargazing tonight, experiencing the sensations that only a sunset or moonbeams can bring to your mind, body, and spirit. Take notice of the stillness in the air, the chill against your skin, the chorus of crickets, the sweet scent of honeysuckle, and the quieting of life all around you. Imagine all the people tucked away safely in their beds, snuggled beneath warm blankets, and drifting off to sleep. Imagine all the dreams that are encircling their unconscious minds, transporting them in time shuttles to distant places, strange lands, and stranger stories. Soon, you'll be there too.

29 COMFORT YOURSELF

How do you treat your own pain? Whether pain is physical, emotional, or situational, too often our inner response is to be angry, judgmental, and rejecting.

This meditation invites you to approach any pain in yourself with compassion and kindness, instead of anger and rejection.

- Breathe mindfully for about a minute.

- Set your intention. For example, "May this practice strengthen my ability to face suffering in myself and others."

- Breathe mindfully for a few more breaths.

- Now, reflect upon a condition or situation in your life that causes you pain.

- Focus on the pain in yourself around this situation. Allow it. Acknowledge your own pain.

- Speak kindly to yourself, as a parent would to an injured child. Say something like "May I be at peace. May I be at ease. May I be free from pain."

- End by opening your eyes and moving gently.

30 RELEASE THIS DAY

While lying in bed and waiting for sleep, if you pay attention to your heart, mind, and body, you may notice patterns of holding onto the events of your day or perhaps even resistance to letting go of them. This can interfere with a good night's sleep. Try taking five good minutes to consciously release your day.

- Breathe or listen mindfully for about a minute.

- Set your intention. For example, "May I release this day and welcome peace and calm within."

- Imagine that your breath moves through all parts of you—your heart (emotions), mind, and body. As your breath moves naturally in and out, imagine that it brings calm and ease and carries away restlessness, stress, and upset.

- Try speaking kindly to any part of you that's in distress, whether physical, emotional, or mental. Say something like "Thank you for all you do; you can rest now. You are released."

- Try speaking to yourself kindly, saying something like "May the highest good come from all my actions today. I release them, and myself. May I be at peace."

- End by breathing or listening mindfully for a few more breaths.

31 CULTIVATE INNER PEACE

For scores of centuries, Taoist practice has observed morning and evening prayers with the belief that evening rites can relax your soul, revitalize your energy, and improve your sleep. Through these daily prayers and meditations, Taoist masters cultivate inner peace with the self and outer peace with the whole world. Take time tonight to say your prayers, to give thanks for your daily blessings, to be open to the adventures that await you, and to nurture peace within yourself.

- While sitting in your bedroom and breathing mindfully and restfully, place both your hands over your heart.

- Say aloud, "Tonight I am following in the footsteps of ancient wise ones. With each breath, I am restoring inner and outer peace, in my heart and in the world."

- In these quiet moments, you are freeing yourself from the negative thoughts and feelings that are obstructing your well-being.

- Say aloud, "I am cultivating lasting wellness within myself. I am extending this goodwill beyond the limits of my body so that it will permeate throughout the world."

32 BODY MANTRA

Even when the workday is behind you, you may find that you experience all of your stored-up pain and muscle tension at the end of the day. While you have a sense of relief to be home, you may feel your neck stiffening or have shooting pains running up and down your back. The following self-hypnosis will guide you in visualizing your body's ability to reduce muscle strain and fatigue. You can do this visualization sitting or standing, whichever is more comfortable.

Take a few slow and relaxing breaths before you begin.

- Scan your body to identify the places where you store your tension—feet, back, arms, shoulders, and so on.

- Once you've located these specific areas, begin training your body to relax by saying, "I am sending peace and comfort throughout my body. When I am in a relaxed state of being, my body works inherently and instinctively to heal my aches and soreness."

- As you begin to feel the release of tension in your body, reaffirm to yourself, "I will feel more alert and refreshed after this mindful practice."

PART 2

APPRECIATING WHO YOU ARE AND WHAT YOU HAVE

We spend so much of our lives caught up in the rat race, constantly striving to achieve the next goal, to climb the ladder, to get to what's next. The five-good-minutes approach allows us time to pause and appreciate who we already are and what we already have. The meditations in this section offer opportunities for personal enrichment, a wiser relationship to our inner life, and growing self-awareness, warmheartedness, and compassion.

33 JOYOUS RAPTURE

Everyone has experienced moments of joy. If joy were a river, we would do everything we could to bathe in it every day. Take five minutes to make a list of the experiences and events that bring you joy, such as fishing, reading, jogging, sewing, spending time with your child, making love, gardening, playing an instrument, singing, doing something nice for someone less fortunate, receiving flowers, doing arts and crafts, surprising a loved one with a gift, winning an award, reaching a goal, talking with a close friend, riding your bicycle, walking through a park, sitting at the beach, eating a ripe peach, having a good belly laugh, feeling the sun on your face, taking an afternoon nap, or playing with your pet...The list goes on and on, much like a river.

When you take note of the little joys in your life, you open yourself to more happiness.

34 REKINDLE THE LIGHT

Each of us has a radiant inner fire of beauty, strength, and wisdom. The problem is we forget how to keep the flame burning. In the dampness of boredom, neglect, or forgetfulness, the fire is extinguished. When you discover this has happened, use the following candle meditation as a guide to rekindle your inner light.

- Start by lighting a candle by your bedside or at your table to accompany you in your morning routine.

- Stare into the flickering flame and imagine the same flame glowing in the center of your soul.

- Imagine this fire as the source of your hope, your dreams, your blessings, and your happiness.

- Feed the flame by offering it protection, compassion, and understanding.

- Remember to acknowledge your inner light daily.

35 OPEN THE DOOR FOR LOVE

At the heart of your desire to be loved is the ability to love yourself, to cherish the good, the not-so-good, and everything else in between. Take this moment to let kind, loving energy shine in on you.

- Make a mental or written list of three physical traits that you love about yourself, such as your smile, hair, and belly.

- Make a mental or written list of three personality traits that you love about yourself, such as your sense of humor, wit, and intellect.

- Now make a final list of three ways that you're good at sharing your love, such as a talent for nurturing others, being a good listener, and the ability to be compassionate.

- By focusing your attention on being loving to yourself, you allow the doors of self-love to open and the warm light of kindness, your own and that of others, to shine into your life.

36 WRITE FROM THE HEART

Your frantically paced life may leave you little time to write your feelings. Take this moment to write yourself a love letter. Through writing, you can channel your love inward. Keep this letter with you as a reminder of the endless well of affection you have for yourself. Here are some suggestions for generating that love note:

- List ten things that you love about yourself.

- Start with "Dear [your name]," and imagine someone madly in love with you whispering into your ear. What kind of romantic expressions would he or she say?

- Write about a selfless and caring act that you did for someone.

- Write the following five times: "I love and cherish you inside and out, each and every day."

- Write the following three times: "You are a magnificent and radiant person. There is only love and compassion here for you."

You can even put this letter in the mail to yourself and open it when you need a boost of self-love.

37 YOUR OWN BEST FRIEND

For many reasons, people tend to omit themselves from any list of their best friends.

What would it feel like to add yourself to that list? Try "befriending" yourself with the following practice:

- Find a place where you can relax without interruption. Breathe mindfully for about a minute.

- Set your intention. For example, "May this practice bring me ease and well-being."

- Visualize yourself sitting with a close friend. Feel your affection for your friend.

- Imagine speaking to him or her warmly, wishing him or her well. You might say, "May you be safe and well" or "May you be happy and healthy."

- Now imagine speaking to yourself with the same feeling. Be as kind to yourself as you are to your friend: "May I be safe and well. May I be happy and healthy."

- Acknowledge and hold with compassion any feelings that arise.

38 TAKE STOCK OF YOUR LIFE

If you are to truly practice living a life of purpose, intention, and gratitude, then you need to take inventory of every conceivable aspect of your life—material, emotional, mental, and spiritual. There's no time like the present to take stock and appraise the contents of your life in terms of their value to you. Ask yourself the following questions to help you get started on your path toward a life of greater meaning, focus, integrity, and appreciation:

- Do my belongings, attitudes, goals, obligations, commitments, relationships, habits, dreams, and wardrobe reflect my values?

- Do they fit my current lifestyle?

- Do they continue to serve me or give me pleasure?

- In what ways do they drain my energy, hinder my happiness, or otherwise not serve me well?

- What are some small changes or adjustments I could make this week to begin the process of weeding out the things that slow me down or diminish my quality of life?

39 DIG YOURSELF OUT OF THE PIT

When you're in the dire pit of despair, it is easy to lose perspective on how fortunate you truly are. For the next few minutes, try this simple exercise to enlarge your perspective.

Begin by broadening the way you view the world. Think of another culture that is very different from your own.

From this larger cultural context, imagine what real day-to-day poverty must feel like.

Imagine that global resources were distributed in such a way that all humans could get their basic needs met. This may require visualizing those with more giving up some of their resources for those with less.

Add up your blessings and be grateful for what you have.

When you open yourself to what others are struggling with, you may find that your own personal problems seem less burdensome and troubling.

40 DREAM ROLL

Dreams can be a window into your subconscious and a source for understanding your deeper self. Follow these simple steps for dream introspection:

Get a dream journal, or a notebook will do, and keep it just for your morning memories.

The next time you wake up, roll over in bed and write down what you were dreaming. Don't get up, or you might lose it. If you don't normally remember your dreams in the morning, take the time to leave a pen and paper by your bed and simply write down your first thoughts upon waking.

- When you write, don't be concerned with punctuation, grammar, or clarity.

- Think back on your dream throughout the day.

- See if you start to remember your dreams the more you write them down.

- See if remembering your dreams adds a sense of renewal and meaning in your life.

Often our morning thoughts are like a cloud bank hazing our vision. Give yourself this time to let the fog settle on the horizon and for your mind to come to a clear and rested awareness.

41 MAY I BE FREE FROM PAIN

Compassion is the opening of your heart to the pain of another.

Have you considered that you could meet any pain in yourself with compassion, instead of anger, fear, or shame?

Use this practice to explore the territory of self-compassion:

- Give yourself some quiet time and space, and breathe mindfully for about a minute.

- Set your intention. For example, "May this practice help me to heal."

- Breathe mindfully for a few more breaths.

- Recall and open to some pain you are carrying. It could be physical, emotional, psychological, or from a relationship— anything.

- Breathe mindfully and stay open to your experience. Allow it to be as it is.

- With kindness and compassion, wish yourself relief and ease. For example, "May I be free from suffering" or "May I be at peace."

- Breathe mindfully, gently repeating your phrase as long as you like.

42 AWARDS PRESENTATION

Judges in your own mind can dominate your inner life. They may say "not good enough" or "not enough" about many of the good things you do. However, these judges are only inner habits of criticism and hostility. They can be retired. This practice will help you establish a different habit—appreciating and honoring yourself and your work.

- Give yourself some privacy and sit quietly.

- Breathe or listen mindfully for about a minute.

- Set your intention. For example, "May this practice help me appreciate myself more."

- Breathe mindfully for a few more breaths.

- Recall a success or something positive you said or did during your day at work recently. See how the good outcome depended on you and your unique gifts.

- Picture giving yourself a beautiful award to acknowledge this good work. Your award includes a sincere thank-you or warm congratulations.

- Allow yourself to open your heart, then step forward to receive your award graciously.

43 INHABIT YOUR KITCHENSCAPE

Hidden treasures live in the ordinary acts of daily life. Their riches can be discovered if you pay attention. Mindfully inhabit the landscape of your kitchen and remain aware throughout the cooking process. Doing so can uncover wonders!

Approach your dinner preparation mindfully, anchoring your attention through mindful breathing or mindful listening as you begin and from time to time as you're cooking.

- Pay mindful attention to your "inner weather" along the way—any sense of hurry, worry, or whatever else you may feel.

- As you proceed, take a mindful breath and acknowledge what you're doing—cutting vegetables or stirring a pot, for example.

- Open yourself to all the sensations, smells, and sounds in the kitchen: See the colors of different ingredients and watch how their colors change as they cook. Hear the sizzling as you add ingredients to a hot pan. Smell the aromas of herbs and spices and feel how comfortable your favorite knife is in your hands. Taste as you go, and consider how cooking changes ingredients in both taste and texture.

- Move intentionally, bring kind attention to the task at hand, and rest in an inner spaciousness as you work. Be present, discover, and enjoy!

44 YOU COME FIRST

Many of us go through life as people pleasers, giving and helping others without taking much time to figure out what we really need to be happy. To recognize what you need, you have to put yourself first. You have to give yourself permission to think for yourself and listen carefully to your inner voice that knows exactly what you need and how to meet that need. It means the next time you catch yourself declining your needs for someone else—such as making plans with someone you really don't want to spend time with—try to stop yourself for just a moment and say, "This isn't what I want and that's okay. I need to do what's best for me."

When in doubt about what you need, you may have a tendency to ask others what they think you should do. Instead, ask yourself the following questions:

"How do I reconnect with my true inner desires, wants, and needs?"

"How can I keep the voice of 'woulda-shoulda-coulda' out of my head?"

"How can I prioritize my needs, making them important and valued, instead of always putting other's needs first?"

It will take some practice, but over time you will gain the skills to put yourself first.

45 GOOD-BYE TO MR. MEAN GUY

Like other patterns of thinking and feeling, self-criticism and meanness become stronger with practice. Frustrations usually trigger the mean self-talk.

Most people don't realize how often or how strongly they practice self-criticism and meanness in their thoughts.

Freedom from such habits, from the inner judges constantly looking to blame, begins with mindfulness of thoughts and feelings and continues with kindness toward yourself.

- When you feel upset, and you recognize voices of self-blame and criticism within, stop and breathe mindfully for about a minute.

- Set your intention. For example, "May this practice free me from the habit of self-criticism."

- Listen more closely and imagine making space for all the negative thoughts. You don't have to fight or argue with them, and you don't have to follow them either. Let them be. Let them go.

- Bring mindfulness to your body. Notice any sensations of tension or holding. Breathe there. Let space open around those sensations.

- As you continue to breathe mindfully, gently ask, "Are those criticisms really true?" "How would I know if they were?" "How would I know if they weren't?" Listen for any answers.

46 FIVE-STAR VALUE

Most of us need to receive some amount of appreciation for the work that we do in our jobs. The best form may come in a pay raise, a letter of appreciation, or a compliment from your supervisor. But what if you feel that others don't value your work? Over time, this perception can be very discouraging, and it can damage your self-esteem. This exercise will boost your sense of self-worth—because when you feel good about yourself, your work as well as your state of mind tend to improve.

Take this moment to first acknowledge all the things you do at work that keep everything flowing smoothly. The things you do may feel small and insignificant to you but they probably aren't in reality. In fact, without you, there might be total chaos—phones ringing off the hook, jammed fax machines, lost files, ignored customers, and so on.

● Close your eyes and remember that appreciation starts from within. Be mindful of giving yourself daily praise: You work hard and have many talents. You are also more than the value of your paycheck. You make an important contribution no matter what you do.

47 LOOK INSIDE

The Japanese practice of self-reflection, *naikan,* can be translated as "inside-looking." *Naikan* offers a profound way of fostering gratitude by focusing on being present in your life rather than feeling trapped in your daily drama and complaints. To practice it, you ask yourself these three questions every day:

- "What have I received today?" Hold sacred space in your mind to remember these blessings throughout your day.

- "What have I given today?" This is your opportunity to acknowledge how you've been generous or helpful to others.

- "What trouble have I caused?" Take this moment to recognize your part in the bigger picture of hidden agendas and daily problems.

While *naikan* may not solve all your problems, it can help to keep things in perspective. When you reflect on your present situation, you step out of the downward spiral of everyday grievances. This practice has the potential to inspire you to be more giving and more grateful.

48 TAKE A FRESH LOOK AT YOURSELF

Because of an inner habit of self-criticism and judgment, we rarely see ourselves accurately, as we are.

This practice invites you to try out a radically different approach to your relationship with yourself. With gratitude, look deeply and mindfully at yourself—being friendly and nonjudgmental.

Breathe mindfully for about a minute.

- Set your intention. For example, "May this practice of self-awareness bring me acceptance and wisdom."

- Breathe mindfully for a few more breaths with your eyes closed.

- Open your eyes and look at yourself in a mirror. Just look without judgment or self-talk. Acknowledge your physical form completely. Reflect how your body supports you in this life.

- Look more deeply. With kindness and compassion, notice your emotional life—fears, hopes, dreams— without judgment.

- Look again. Acknowledge a source of inspiration, wonder, beauty, mystery, or surprise within you— with gratitude.

- End by breathing deeply once or twice and moving gently.

49 CIRCLE OF LOVE

Difficult times in your life create obstacles to opening yourself to love. The following visualization will help you create a beaming circle of love that will radiate inward and outward throughout your day.

Imagine you are lying comfortably in a safe and undisturbed place, such as your bedroom or a peaceful meadow. You are free of worries and constraints, deadlines and demands. You are relaxed and calm.

Now, visualize a golden light encircling your whole body. The light represents all the love there is in the world. The light is warm and soothing, comforting and reassuring. The light is like a healing balm to past relationship wounds, to the loss of a loved one, to grief. The light holds the power to calm volatile emotions, such as anger, resentment, and fear. It has the ability to mend broken hearts and repair damaged personal connections.

Take this moment to visualize the healing nature of your love. Do you feel more serene, uplifted, happy? Remind yourself daily that your love circle surrounds you at all times. You simply need to bring it to mind for it to work its healing magic.

50 GET UNGLUED

Everyone has experienced feeling trapped—stuck in a job you hate, trapped in an unhealthy relationship, or confined to a lifestyle that has you up to your ears in unwanted debt. You almost feel as if you've been permanently glued to something from which you can't escape. Take the next five minutes to work on getting unstuck from these pressures. Even if there are no simple solutions to your immediate situation, imagine that alternatives await you, if you are patient and open to receiving them. Contemplate the prospect that you may be happy with a different arrangement. Ask yourself the following questions to get a sense of your choices and options:

"Why do I feel stuck or trapped?"

"Do I really need these things in order to be happy?"

"Could I find fulfillment in other ways, given the opportunity?"

"What small changes could I make now that might slowly give me the space that I need to find more contentment in my life?"

51 BITE BY SAVORY BITE

So often we eat mindlessly while reading or watching television, or even while driving. Eating mindfully and with particular attention to the simple act of chewing can be a vital way of connecting more deeply with your body and your health. Conscious eating means putting aside all distractions and enjoying your meal with the full awareness of all your senses—sight, sound, smell, texture, and taste—and being aware of every movement you make.

Begin by taking three deep, relaxed breaths when you're seated before your meal.

- Notice the way you hold your eating utensils. Are you right-handed or left-handed?

- What would you like your first bite to consist of? The salad? The main entrée? The side dish?

- Observe how much food you have on your fork. Notice its shapes, textures, and colors.

- Which aromas in this meal are most pleasing to you? What do they remind you of?

- As you take this first bite, eat slowly and methodically, chewing at least twenty times before you swallow.

- Take the time to savor every bite and fully experience all the taste sensations.

At the end of this experience, consider how you feel. Sated? Grateful? What was it like to eat your meal in this way?

52 ONE-WAY TICKET TO THE MOON

Each of us carries around some emotional burdens that we would like to discard. Wouldn't it be great if you could simply pack up all of your emotional baggage, purchase a one-way ticket to send the suitcase to the moon, and then throw a good-riddance party? Forgive yourself today. Take the next few minutes to complete the following forgiveness exercises. Fill in the blanks.

"Today is a good day to forgive myself for _____."

"I can be hard on myself when I _____, so today I am letting it go."

"I'm still mad at myself for _____, but today I am forgiving and forgetting."

"For all those years that I held on to the pain of _____, today I am freeing myself and feeling exonerated."

Give yourself a free ticket to forgiveness. Let go of the weight of your troubles and ease your mind.

53 HARMONIZE WITH REALITY

A half-glance at mainstream commercial media will reveal society's obsession with staying young forever. But you don't have to play into that beauty myth. Because no one can escape the natural aging process, prepare yourself to wholeheartedly embrace it with dignity and grace, and to recognize its splendor! To harmonize with reality means challenging yourself to learn how to be joyful, or at least carefree, about wrinkles, gray hair, a slowing gait, and declining strength.

- Take this moment to acknowledge the life force of ageless beauty that starts from within you and radiates outward through every smile, every act of kindness, and the breath of every generous spirit.

- Say aloud your affirmation several times: "I am a gorgeous, attractive, and magnificent being, inside and out, head to toe." Remember, you are not the sum of your aging body parts.

- Assume the stature of royalty in this moment and be aware of your posture. Walk tall with pride for who you really are, and move with ease.

54 APPRECIATE YOURSELF

All too often we focus on what is wrong about ourselves instead of what is right. The consequences of such imbalance include enormous pain and fear.

This practice invites you to restore some balance through mindful attention and appreciation.

- Breathe mindfully for about a minute.

- Set your intention. For example, "May this practice of appreciation quiet self-judgment and criticism in me."

- Breathe mindfully for a few more breaths, and then bring attention to a part of your body. Reflect on how it functions and supports your life. For example, lungs support breathing, feet transport you, eyes enable seeing.

- As you focus, offer your body part a gentle thank-you. Now, move on to another part.

- Extend this practice to a quality about yourself, such as loyalty, courage, intelligence, or generosity. Thank that part also.

- Continue to reflect, thanking yourself for your body and inner qualities for a few more minutes.

- End by opening your eyes and moving gently.

55 BEFRIEND YOURSELF

Feelings of ease and peace, including a sense of safety, are wonderful allies for restful sleep. These feelings flow from your deep capacity for kindness and acceptance. It's important to remember that no matter what may happen in the outer world, you can always offer yourself those gifts of kindness and acceptance.

This practice can help you remember how to befriend yourself and, in so doing, to foster warm feelings of well-being that can help ease you into sleep.

- Breathe or listen mindfully for about a minute.

- Set your intention. For example, "May this practice bring me peace and a good night's sleep."

- Breathe or listen mindfully for a few more breaths.

- Imagine speaking quietly to yourself, as you would speak to a dear friend, with kindness and acceptance.

- Wish yourself well, using words or phrases that speak to you on a deep level. For example, you might say, "May I be safe and filled with peace," "May I be happy and at ease," or "May I be healed and healthy."

- Repeat this phrase for as long as you like.

- End by resting quietly in silence.

56 A SHOT OF FAITH

Faith is a concept that means different things to different people. Used here, faith simply means the understanding that life is a mystery and living in the mystery is what life is all about. Life is full of "what ifs" and "whys." Each of us has core beliefs about life, love, and the principles that guide us in how we live. For the next five minutes, take an imaginary journey to connect with your inner, personal faith. Start this visualization with three deep breaths. Imagine that you have come to the edge of all that you know and are about to step off into the dark of the unknown.

- Think of a challenge you are facing in your life at this time.

- What are your thoughts, fears, or concerns?

- Now visualize that same challenge working out perfectly.

- Notice how different it feels to let go and to have faith that you have everything it takes in life to face that challenge.

- Believing in yourself gives you strength and resiliency.

57 NO MORE GRUMPY MORNINGS

Here is an antidote for waking up grumpy. Try writing down all the good things that happened to you over the past week. It's not always as easy as you might think. But by making a mental list of a couple of sweet moments, you can sweep away your negativity and replace it with gratitude. Here are some suggestions to help trigger your memory:

- A neighbor complimented you on your blouse.

- A friend called to thank you for something you did to help out.

- A stranger insisted that you go ahead of him at a long check-out line at the market.

- You saw a small child trying to take some wobbly steps, and it made you smile inside.

- You noticed that one of your houseplants has just started to blossom.

- Someone smiled at you on the way to work.

The smallest act or the briefest occasion is all it takes to remind you of the beauty in your life.

58 HONOR YOUR COMMITMENTS

Take a few minutes to make a mental or written list of five commitments that you would like to make to yourself and for yourself today. Here are some examples to help you get started:

"I am committed to doing the best I can today, and my best is good enough."

"I am committed to giving and receiving more love every day."

"I am committed to addressing my health issues and learning new ways to promote my wellbeing."

"I am committed to making new friends."

"I am committed to making time in my schedule for an exercise program."

Commitments are challenging but rewarding. Setting goals gives you direction, focus, and intention in your life. And when you make the effort to list your goals, you activate your potential for achievement.

59 FREE YOUR HEART

Your past can haunt you and sabotage your ability to feel lovable. Old emotional wounds from past breakups or traumas can be obstacles to remaining open to love. Taking a self-nurturing five minutes to heal old wounds will help you give and receive the loving-kindness that you truly desire.

When you find those painful losses and hurtful emotions stomping around loudly in your life, let them be your signal to be gentle with your heart.

Acknowledge your past wounds by making a mental or written list of a few hurtful occasions.

Go down your list and recite a healing prayer for forgiveness for each and every situation. Say aloud or to yourself: "Through this ritual of forgiveness, I am freeing myself from past wrongs and injuries. I am showering my old heartache with compassion to set me free to give and receive abundant love."

60 SELF-PRESERVATION FIRST

Your work or home life may demand a lot of you. Your high level of responsibility may force you to be under the gun for time and pressured to drop whatever you're doing in order to do something else. This can put your mind and body into a tailspin of stress and anxiety. You may have skipped a meal or forgotten to meet your basic needs before you rushed off to work. Self-care doesn't come easily for most people, but it is a necessary part of restoring a sense of well-being and good health. Take a few minutes to unwind from this frantic momentum with the intention of self-preservation.

● Begin by making a mental list of your basic human needs for each and every day of your life, such as water, shelter, food, warmth, clothes, and so on.

● Take note of the things that you ignored while you scurried to meet work demands. Did you forget to drink water today? When was your last sit-down meal? Did you skip the gym?

- What can you do in this moment that would enable you to take better care of yourself? For example, keep your body hydrated, order food to be delivered, or wash your hands and face to cool your frayed nerves.

In the future, consider always keeping a water bottle with you or packing some snacks before you leave the house.

61 LOWER YOUR STANDARDS

If you set high standards for yourself in regard to fulfilling the needs of others, then "no" can be the hardest word in your vocabulary to verbalize. You may suffer from feelings of terrible guilt or anxiety when yet another everyday obligation leaps into your path. It takes tremendous determination and practice to relax your standards. But learning to say no may save your life; it may rescue you from the unceasing clutches of a life overburdened with too many obligations, extra side projects, invitations, and unnecessary deadlines that steal away your precious energy and time.

Take a few moments to exercise your freedom to say no to things that zap your energy. Saying no will bolster your self-respect and your ability to put your needs first. Remind yourself that it's never too late to call someone back and say, "Something unexpected came up and I can't make it. Thanks for thinking of me." Or you might say, "Thanks for the invitation, but it conflicts with other plans." This is true: those "other" plans are for taking care of you.

62 FEEL GRATITUDE FOR THIS DAY

Restful sleep is promoted by feelings of well-being and ease at bedtime. Unfortunately, your mind may often habitually dwell on negative or worrisome topics just when rest is near.

This simple practice of gratitude can help shift your experience from worry to ease.

- Lying in bed, breathe or listen mindfully for about a minute.

- Set your intention. For example, "May this practice free my heart and mind for restful sleep."

- Breathe or listen mindfully for a few more breaths.

- Recall and reflect on one good thing that happened or came to you this day. Relax, take some time, and open deeply to the experience. Feel the good wishes, the support, and the security that you received from this gift.

- If you become aware of more things you're grateful for, feel their goodness deeply too.

- Let go of any critical judgments, comments, or stories about the things you're grateful for.

- Rest in the goodness and say thank you.

63 EFFORTLESS SIMPLICITY

Simplifying a few minor things in your home can make space for inner peace and happiness. Simplicity is the key to achieving lasting harmony. Let's begin with an effortless mental visualization. Start with a picture of your home in your mind. Imagine each room fitting a perfect ideal of a spiritually comforting space. Sunshine is bursting forth from every window. Each room is pleasant, uncluttered, and tidy. Your favorite comfy chair is propped with pillows. Even your plants seem to welcome you when you come in the door. There is a feeling of calmness in every corner. This is your safe haven from a world of chaos. Now make a mental or written wish list for what you could do to achieve this ideal space. Here are some ideas to get you started:

Fill one bag with clothes and shoes that you haven't worn in years. Give them away.

Fill a box with books you no longer need.

Fill a bag with old magazines and newspapers for recycling.

Box up any remaining half-finished projects from years ago that you're never going to complete.

Clutter in the home brings clutter in your personal life. Clear away some clutter, and you'll be surprised what a relief it can bring.

64 CULTIVATE CURIOSITY

Studies show that there is a link between curiosity and well-being. In fact, highly curious people report greater satisfaction with life. If you know someone who's obsessed with a hobby, whether it's quilting or car restoration, then you're familiar with how highly motivated he or she can be with a project. What you might not know is that curiosity can be cultivated, even when you're not feeling motivated.

Begin by working with what you have. Unbury those old treasures stored away that used to inspire you, such as a musical instrument, arts and crafts projects, or your tennis racket.

- Schedule a time on your calendar to reconnect with the enjoyment you experienced with these activities.

- When you start a project, don't focus on the outcome or the final product. Instead, pay attention to the process. This exploration isn't a contest or race to the finish line, so just enjoy this moment in your self-discovery.

- Try something new! Invite a friend to participate in pursuing a new interest that seems intimidating, such as painting or martial arts.

- Make a pact with yourself that you're going to follow through on this pursuit and not criticize yourself.

- Developing a sense of wonder can bring greater meaning to your life.

65 AN OUNCE OF APPRECIATION

One way to loosen the vise grip that stress has on your life is to soften to the beauty all around you, opening your heart and mind to the kindness and joy that other people and pets bring to your life. It's harder to stay frustrated and angry when you're busy focusing on the goodness that surrounds you. This practice invites you to keep a running mental or written list of what you appreciate about your family, friends, pets, and even yourself. Here are some ideas for the types of things your list might include:

I am a strong and resilient person and have survived difficult times with dignity and grace.

- I'm lucky to have generous and caring people in my life.

- I'm grateful that my partner loves me despite my flaws and shortcomings.

- My best friend has a great sense of humor, which helps me to lighten up and laugh.

- My pet reminds me daily that I am loved and needed.

PART 3

CONNECTING TO OTHERS AND THE WORLD AROUND YOU

So often we take friends, family, and coworkers for granted. In this section, you will find meditations and exercises to help you hear others more accurately, respond to them more thoughtfully, and relate to them more compassionately. You will also learn to connect with your surroundings in a more curious and appreciative way, deepening your relationship to the world around you. These practices remind us that we are continually in relationship to all things, and by noticing and gently exploring this broader context for love, the depth of feeling for any single person or creature grows.

66 EXERCISE YOUR KINDNESS MUSCLES

Most people know that feelings—anger, happiness, sadness, and fear, for example—are not permanent. They come and they go.

What most people don't realize is that such feelings are like muscles. They can actually be strengthened by deliberate exercise! For example, dwelling on anger and hurt actually makes those feelings stronger. But the same goes for feelings like happiness and kindness.

So, try strengthening the feeling of kindness in your life, instead of anger.

This practice is an easy way to exercise your kindness "muscles."

- Breathe mindfully for about a minute.

- Set your intention. For example, "May this practice awaken greater feelings of kindness in me."

- Think of someone you know—a friend or coworker perhaps. Imagine speaking directly to that person in a kind voice. You could say something like "May you be safe and peaceful" or "May you be happy and healthy." Really get behind the phrase, putting all of your energy there.

- Repeat your word or phrase gently, in your own heart, over and over, like a lullaby.

- Try speaking to yourself with the same kindness.

67 CONNECT WITH SOUND

Close attention to sounds—listening deeply—can awaken a sense of connection to life and access to an experience of vast interior spaciousness. This practice is a way to explore your connection to life through sounds. Try it indoors and outdoors.

- Breathe mindfully for about a minute.

- Set your intention. For example, "May deep listening reveal richness and awe in my life."

- Breathe mindfully for a few more breaths.

- Shift attention from your breath to the sounds around you, paying attention to them and allowing them, without judgment or preference, to be there.

- Listen to all that reveals itself: soft, loud, pleasing, annoying, even to the space between the sounds. Welcome each sound with deep attention.

- Listen for a few more minutes. End by opening your eyes and moving gently.

68 NATURE'S GIFT TO YOU

Nature is bountiful and plentiful, and yet we often forget to take notice of nature's simple gifts of joy and serenity. Take five minutes, and like the old saying goes...

Stop and smell the flowers.

Notice the flight of a bumblebee.

Listen to the rustle of the wind through the trees.

Take in the majestic beauty of a mountain range, if there's one nearby. Or just consider the beauty of whatever kind of nature surrounds you.

Smell the salty scent of the sea air, if that's nearby.

Look up at the clouds and the sky.

Keep a mindful awareness and appreciation of all the beauty that surrounds you in each moment. When you take this time to open your senses to the pleasures of what is just outside your door, whatever that happens to be, you open your mind and body to nature's restorative power to soothe and heal you.

69 APPRECIATE A LOVED ONE

We are constantly receiving blessings and the benefits of love and support from others. Yet how often do we stop to acknowledge them?

This practice invites deeper appreciation for the gifts of others and what they add to your inner and outer life.

- Breathe mindfully for about a minute.

- Set your intention. For example, "May this practice deepen my connection with _____ [say your loved one's name here]."

- Breathe mindfully for a few breaths. Now picture the loved one you wish to appreciate.

- Reflect on his or her positive presence in your life. Whisper a quiet thank you.

- Reflect on how this person has supported you. Say thank you.

- Reflect on how this person has loved you. Say thank you.

- End by breathing mindfully for a few breaths.

- The next time you speak with your loved one, thank him or her.

70 GIVE IT AWAY

Love comes to us when we give it away. In fact, the more love you give, the more love you have to give. Right now, take five minutes to share your love. Make the most of it, and be generous! Here are some suggestions to get you started:

- Plan a meal that will be infused with your love.

- Write a love note to someone you care about and copy the same note for yourself.

- Call someone dear to you and tell that person how much you love them. Then call yourself and leave a message declaring your love for yourself.

- Give a gift or something meaningful to a friend or stranger, or donate money or clothes to a charity.

- Practice being generous and patient with your coworkers, customers, the cashier-clerk, and the driver with road rage.

- Be loving with a stranger by offering a smile, saying hello, wishing them a nice day, or giving them a compliment.

When you make others feel good, it has a magical way of making you feel good.

71 SILENT HARMONY

Throughout the ages, great spiritual philosophers have encouraged people to align themselves with peace and love. Unfortunately, there is little peace on our planet. Take this meditative moment to be mindful of how cultivating serenity within yourself can attract harmony in the world.

- While seated comfortably, quietly take a few deep breaths. On the inhale, take in the calm and serenity that you desire. On the exhale, let go of the turmoil and madness of the world.

- Let the noises of your mind drift off. Let your cluttered thoughts and everyday distractions dissipate. You are safe and free to leave your fears and worries behind.

- Imagine opening a door within your heart to infinite peace and harmony. Be aware of the power of your inner peace as a magnet for tranquility in the world around you. May it be so.

72 THE PULSE OF LIFE

Nobel peace laureate Bishop Desmond Tutu, in his writing, shared an ancient African term with our Western culture: *ubuntu*, which encompasses the concept of who we are within the global community. *Ubuntu* is the essence of all humanity. Western culture thinks almost exclusively in terms of "I" at the unfortunate loss of "we." You can learn to expand your notions of "I" to include "we." Take the next five minutes to see yourself in the greater web of life, intertwined with each and every person, plant, and species on earth. Your existence is inextricably interwoven with their existence. When we can step out of our individualized and compartmentalized lives, we free ourselves to see the bigger picture, to feel more connected with the intoxicating pulse of life and all its wonder. To belong in the greater goodness of all life can bring perspective and compassion into your spirit on a daily basis.

73 BLESSINGS TO YOU

Do you have someone in your life whom you find hard to love? Perhaps this person is emotionally shut down or difficult to connect with. Try this blessing prayer. It may surprise you with wonderful and unexpected results.

- Make a mental or written list of three things about that person that you don't like.

- Now make a mental or written list of three things about that person that you do like.

- After each item listed, say aloud a prayer to bless that person for all that is good and all that is complicated in them. You may want to speak their name aloud, followed by: "For all the difficult parts of you, I bless you. I bless you and wish that only love and joy fills your heart." Follow this with: "For all the gentle and kind parts of you, I bless you. I bless you and wish you abundant happiness every day."

The blessing prayer works best with practice on a daily basis. Over time, it can have astonishing outcomes.

141

74 DEAR FRIENDS AND COLLEAGUES

Like all other relationships, workplace relationships involve some friction. Could your inner relationship to a coworker impact both of you? This practice invites you to experiment with the inner relationship. Notice when this practice begins to affect the outer relationship.

- Breathe or listen mindfully for about a minute.

- Set your intention. For example, "May this practice strengthen my work relationships."

- Think of someone you work with whom you like.

- Imagine speaking to that person in a friendly way, wishing them well, saying, "May you be happy," "May you be safe," or something similar.

- Now think of someone you work with who is difficult.

- Imagine speaking to this person in the same friendly way, using your kind words. You aren't excusing this person's bad behavior, you're just practicing friendliness.

- End by being quiet. Notice, honor, and learn from all of your feelings and reactions to this practice.

75 AFFECTIONATE LISTENING

How often is your attention elsewhere when your partner is speaking?

A deeper connection and more joy are close at hand when you replace inattention with affectionate listening.

- When your partner is speaking to you, notice where your attention is. Notice also any feelings of impatience or mental "stories" that may be going through your head. Acknowledge them and let them go.

- Take a moment to breathe mindfully for a few breaths.

- Set your intention. For example, "May I be more present for _____ [name of person]."

- As your partner speaks to you, focus mindfully on the sounds. Notice tone, pace, and volume, as well as meaning.

- Look more closely at your partner. If you are on a phone, close your eyes and picture him or her.

- As you listen, let gentle feelings of warmth and affection flow within you.

- Let attention and affection guide your own words in response.

76 THE HOMESTRETCH

Imagine if your commute home from work could be like window shopping; each passing store front, sidewalk, garden, car, and pedestrian would become a stroll through a museum. Visualize the freeway as an architectural monument and consider every building a structural splendor, eliciting awe and wonder. Notice every shrub or tree and imagine if we had a word for every shade of green. Your journey home is an opportunity to see the world as if for the first time. You may notice extraordinary things that you never saw before, such as a stained-glass window, school children hugging, or a smile from a passing stranger.

After work, set your mind at ease and immerse yourself in the sights and sounds of your neighborhood. Remember to relax, breathe, and enjoy this passage into your evening. This is the perfect time to detach from the burdens of your job and observe the people and places along your path home. Let the sights and sounds quiet your mind. By the time you return home, you'll feel renewed and ready for whatever awaits you.

77 WHERE HAPPINESS LIVES

Foreground: what dominates your attention.

Background: everything else.

When worries or stressful situations grow large and loud, they tend to dominate the foreground of your experience in every moment. A simple, mindful shift of focus from foreground to background can illuminate the many places where happiness still lives—even in distressing moments.

- Breathe or listen mindfully for about a minute.

- Set your intention. For example, "May this practice bring peace and balance to my life."

- Breathe or listen mindfully. Name any worries or problems in the foreground of your awareness. Let them be.

- Deliberately shift your attention from those worries to your background, to your surrounding environment. See, hear, and sense all that is around you.

- Acknowledge and appreciate the sources of beauty and happiness around you: loved ones, pets, plants, beautiful objects—all of it.

- Open yourself to any feelings of joy and gratitude that begin to arise in you.

78 JOY IS US TOGETHER

When you are with your partner or with dear family members (including pets), allow yourself to connect to and drink deeply of the preciousness in that moment. Try this practice to help you step back from the distraction of inner busyness and relax into the love that surrounds you:

- Whatever your posture, gently and quietly begin to breathe mindfully.

- Set your intention. For example, "May I feel the love around me in this moment."

- Breathe mindfully for a few more breaths.

- Notice any sense of worry, hurry, impatience, or ill ease in your inner life. Acknowledge it kindly and let it go.

- If it helps, gently remind yourself where you are. For example: "This moment, here with those who love me."

- Look and feel more deeply. Rest in the love you feel.

79 TAKE A HIKE

With today's sedentary lifestyle, we often don't get enough exercise. But even a short, gentle stroll can alleviate pent-up stress and remind you of the healing force of moving your body. Just before lunch, give yourself permission to get outside and go for a walk, take a hike, or jog around the nearby vicinity. The fresh air alone will do you some good.

- On your walk, take five minutes to be mindful of your natural surroundings—the birds, plants, insects, wind, and clouds. Even if you work in the middle of a city, the natural world is all around you.

- With each step, you are distancing yourself from all your work obligations and stress. You are leaving behind your extra burden.

- With each breath, notice the world around you— people, places, sculptures, and parks.

- When it comes time to return, with every step you take toward your job site, become increasingly aware of the calming power of being outside.

80 LOOKING AT YOU

How often do you look at your loved ones without really seeing them?

Such a failure to connect is usually the result of your attention being focused elsewhere.

Try the following practice of "mindful seeing" to renew and strengthen your connection.

- When you are with your loved one, notice if you are really present and paying attention or not.

- If you are not paying attention, calmly acknowledge that without judging yourself.

- Quietly set your intention to connect.

- Breathe mindfully for a few breaths if it helps steady your attention.

- Look gently and more closely at your loved one. See them through eyes of kindness and interest. Notice skin, eyes, hair, expression, clothing, and body posture. Keep breathing mindfully, and relax as you notice more and more.

- How do you feel? Be kind to yourself, too.

- What will happen next?

81 STARS OF COMPASSION

The Dalai Lama believes that if you meditate on compassion for others, the first beneficiary will be you. And the Buddha believed that when you love yourself, you cannot bring harm to another. Compassion starts with you. It is a steady reminder that others are also suffering, and so you are not alone. This meditation will guide you along your path toward greater empathy and happiness.

- What does compassion mean to you? Reflect on what it means to have empathy, understanding, and concern for others. For some, it is an empathetic awareness of the complexity of difficult situations and the complicated feelings that arise.

- Consider a time when you were compassionate. Did you comfort someone after a painful breakup? Did you make a donation to a natural-disaster relief organization?

- What emotions are you experiencing right now? Openheartedness? Sympathy? Love?

- Now consider a time when someone showed compassion toward you. Perhaps a friend gave extra emotional support during a tender time in your life.

These are the stars of compassion that light our path along our journey toward happiness.

82 NO PAIN, NO BLAME

Have you ever noticed how often the desire to blame someone arises from your own feelings of pain and upset?

While responsibility and accountability are vital in healthy relationships, unfair criticism and blame are toxic.

Try the following practice the next time you feel hurt and want to blame someone:

- Breathe or listen mindfully for about a minute.

- Include your body sensations in your mindful attention. Notice especially your throat, chest, and abdomen.

- Let your attention be filled with kindness and compassion.

- Set your intention. For example, "May my pain not drive me to harm another."

- Breathe, listen, or notice sensations mindfully for a few more breaths.

- Notice any angry or blaming thoughts or stories you may be having. Let them go. Stop feeding or following them. Don't blame yourself for any thoughts you may have either.

- Decide on the wisest action only after attending to your own pain.

83 THE EXTRAORDINARY IN THE ORDINARY

Our everyday routines can get drab. If you watch enough television, it can appear as though everyone is having the time of their lives, a lifetime full of one adventure after another. This exercise is about finding the miraculous in daily life, searching for the unique in the mundane, or imagining the unimaginable. Today, take five minutes to observe the less noticeable things in the morning:

- the sound of baby birds chirping just outside your window

- the wind rustling through the trees

- the smile on a baby's face

Find fascination in something that others might shrug off. Look at the world with new eyes. Take notice of the little things. Life is brimming over with wondrous and spectacular happenings right under your nose. You simply need to open yourself to the precious moments that can provide insight and perspective throughout the rest of your day.

84 A DOSE OF ADMIRATION

While you're still lying in bed, take five minutes to acknowledge the people who have been most influential or inspiring in your life. Take this time to acknowledge that you have a blessed life. Life is a gift. People have been generous and changed your life. Consider the following questions:

Whom do you admire?

What qualities do you admire in them?

What was the best advice that you ever received from them?

How could you embody the qualities that you admire the most in others?

Sit with these answers and acknowledge what feelings surface for you. Take the time to nurture these endearing qualities in yourself throughout the day.

85 FIND JOY IN ANOTHER'S GOOD FORTUNE

Does another's good fortune (a vacation, promotion, engagement) ever make you feel jealous or envious, or somehow less than? Have you noticed how these negative feelings seem to leave you more irritable, isolated, and lonely, not less?

This practice, sympathetic joy, is a powerful way to turn away from feelings of insecurity and separation and toward the inherent joy and connection possible in each situation.

- Breathe mindfully for about a minute.

- Set your intention. For example, "May this practice support my relationship with others and diminish feelings of envy and doubt in myself."

- Sit quietly and think of someone you know who has enjoyed good fortune recently.

- For the next few minutes, imagine speaking to this person, sensing their joy, and saying something to wish them well—like "May your good fortune never end" or "May you always be happy."

- Whenever other thoughts or feelings arise in you, kindly let them go and return to the phrases you have selected.

- End by opening your eyes and moving gently.

86 COMPASSIONATE COMMUNICATION

Communication is central to any relationship, whether it's between you and your partner, a friend, or a coworker. Cultivate the good listener in yourself with this next exercise.

- When a conversation first starts to break down or become confusing, resist the familiar temptation to get angry and frustrated. Your stress may lead to raised voice levels or an unkind tone of voice, which rarely helps anyone feel understood.

- Instead, try to consciously activate your compassionate side or the active good listener inside yourself. This starts with being patient and giving the other person fair and adequate time to speak. You may nod or ask questions, but do your best not to interrupt.

- Observe your breathing pattern, and be mindful of each breath returning you to a state of patience and understanding.

- Repeat back what you believe you heard the other person say, which will convey that you were listening and care about that person's opinions.

The act of compassionate listening takes practice and doesn't come easily on the first try, but the benefits will encourage a renewed feeling of camaraderie and solidarity.

87 ALTAR OF LOVE

A great many places of worship contain altars or sacred spaces for ornaments to reside and where ceremonies are performed. Why not create one in your home as a symbol of your magical connection with loved ones?

- Keep it simple and small—perhaps just a tiny box covered in colorful cloth with a single candle on your mantel, with a photo that represents togetherness or that makes your heart smile inside.

- Each night before you sleep, light the candle alone or with someone you love and recognize the inherent beauty of your altar for love. Consider what it means to take this tranquil time to honor your loving relationships.

- Speak your intentions: "I light this candle to remind me that I am blessed with loving people in my life."

May your altar be a guidepost that always leads back to your openness to love and gratitude.

88 FIND THE OCEAN IN A SEASHELL

As a child, you may have been told that you can hear the ocean inside a conch shell, if you really listen. There was something magical and wonderful and mysterious about this discovery. When your routine starts to get drab and mundane, discover the wonder hidden in secret places of your imagination.

Find an inanimate object to examine. It could be anything—a spool of thread, a chair, a tree.

Scan for parts of it that are simple as well as complex, ordinary as well as extraordinary. For example, your window is made of simple clear glass that's been cut into a square, but it is marvelous how the sunlight shines through, enveloping the room with its glimmering rays of warmth. Now you try it!

Do the same exercise with your relationship, noticing the components that are plain as well as astonishing.

Stir up the extraordinary in every part of your life. This new outlook just might inspire you.

89 THAT OBNOXIOUS PERSON AND YOU

Here that person comes again! You know who—that obnoxious one. That person is not fun, not agreeable, and definitely not pleasant.

The interaction leaves you filled with ill will, distress, even outrage.

But remember, you can protect yourself and set the upset down.

- During the interaction, use mindful breathing to anchor and support yourself.

- At times, offer a silent affirmation. For example, "I am wise and strong enough to handle this situation."

- As you listen to that person's words, see how he or she is trying to be happy too, just like everyone else.

- As you look at that person, imagine him or her as a child. What pain did he or she suffer?

- When you speak, try wishing that person happiness. For example, "I'm sorry to hear that. I hope things get better."

- Protect yourself. Mindfully set limits and disengage respectfully.

- As you leave that person, turn your attention and open heart to your next breath.

90 FEEL YOUR CONNECTION WITH ALL THINGS

Using phrases linked to the process of inhaling and exhaling, this practice offers the opportunity to explore your connections in the web of life.

- Breathe mindfully for about a minute.

- Set your intention. For example, "May this practice open my heart more deeply."

- Focus attention on your breath.

Link silent phrases with each in-breath and out-breath as follows:

"Breathing in, I feel breath supporting my life."

"Breathing out, I say thank you for being alive."

"Breathing in, I know all living things must breathe."

"Breathing out, I feel my connection with all living things."

"Breathing in, I wish happiness and peace for myself."

"Breathing out, I see that all living things wish happiness and peace."

Explore linking breath to any other phrases that appeal to you.

91 A CHILD'S EYES

Have you ever noticed how remarkable life is through a child's eyes? Everything is a wonder to be explored. Children often ask a hundred questions about the simplest and most complex things in everyday life. Imagine cultivating some of that wonder and amazement in your consciousness. Life becomes full of questions, full of excitement and endless fascination.

Take the next few minutes to focus on something in your room or just outside your window.

Pretend you are looking at it through a child's eyes.

Take notice of how a child might perceive what you're looking at.

Ask yourself very simple questions like these: "What is that?" "How did it get there?" "What is it for?"

When you can recapture your childhood innocence, you remember what is really important in life. You can recall the simple things. You awaken your deeply buried amazement, fascination, bewilderment, and amusement.

92 OFFER FORGIVENESS

As human beings in relationships, we inevitably hurt each other, intentionally or unintentionally. That is why forgiveness is so important. When another person hurts you, you have the choice of holding resentment or offering forgiveness. Forgiveness is "offered" because you have no control over whether or not the other will accept it. Offering forgiveness is not an invitation for the other to hurt you again but is instead a means of releasing your own hurt. You can explore offering forgiveness with this practice.

Breathe or listen mindfully for about a minute.

- Set your intention. For example, "May I learn more about forgiveness."

- Recall a time when someone hurt you.

- Imagine speaking to them, saying, "I offer you forgiveness."

- Repeat this phrase several times and notice your own inner responses.

- What did you learn? What needs to happen next?

93 REST IN BEAUTY

When you are feeling closed off, isolated, or alone, relief is closer than you might think. Learn to restore and reconnect by resting in beauty. Your key to connection lies in mindful attention to the fullness and beauty of life around you.

Stop whatever you are doing and practice mindful breathing, listening, or movement for about a minute.

- Set your intention. For example, "May this practice of attention to beauty revitalize me."

- Continue mindfulness practice for a few more breaths.

- Look around you. Notice beauty. See it in color, shape, space, motion. When you find something beautiful, look closer. Rest there.

- Listen mindfully. Find the beauty in sounds. Hear the tones, rhythm, and silence.

- Find beauty around you using your other senses—smell, taste, touch.

- Rest in all the beauty around you.

94 YOUR FAMILY CIRCLE

There can be great power in remembering and acknowledging your extended family and the common bonds running, literally, as blood through your veins. Which talents, interests, even foibles are shared with ancestors and relations? Visiting your "family circle" mindfully can feed a deeper appreciation of your connection to life too.

Breathe or listen mindfully for about a minute.

- Set your intention. For example, "May this practice enrich and nurture me."

- Reflect gently on a specific talent or gift of yours.

- Recall a relative or ancestor who shared that gift. Imagine he or she is with you.

- Think of other gifts or qualities you possess. Imagine a circle of your family members surrounding you, whenever you need them, sharing gifts, strengths, and challenges.

- Feel their presence and support deep in your veins.

95 DUMP THE GRUDGE

"I can never forgive him for what happened at Thanksgiving three years ago." You know with absolute certainty that you're holding a grudge when you can recall the exact date, time, and location of a hurtful episode that unleashed your resentment. You also know that grudges are toxic, negative energy that can grow over time and fuel disharmony. Here's a mindful opportunity to liberate your grudges in order to allow the love to flow more freely from within. Make a brief mental or written list of the people toward whom you carry resentment.

- These longstanding bitter feelings may be closely attached to a painful memory. Pay attention to the feelings and sensations that arise for you when you revisit that painful memory, person, or situation. Do you feel sadness, shame, or anger? Do you notice any tension mounting in your body, such as in your neck, shoulders, or stomach?

- Reconnect with the rhythm of your breathing and observe.

- Say aloud: "I am ready to let go of my grudges in this moment in time. I am ready to reopen myself to more love and more compassion for the things that I cannot change today." Feel free to repeat these words, or your own words, several times over, until they come naturally and comfortably.

- This exercise works best when practiced for five minutes each day. The effects will surprise you.

96 THE PET WHO LOVES YOU

With a bark, a purr, a bounce, a wiggle, or a moving tail, your pet lets you know how happy they are to see you. Try taking five good minutes to really be with your loving friend.

Engaging with your pet, pay attention mindfully to what's happening.

- Let yourself receive the experience as it unfolds, noticing your inner sense of joy, love, excitement, or anything else you may feel.

- Notice the way your pet moves, hear the sounds they make, feel the texture of their fur, gaze at their face and into their eyes.

- Open yourself to the give-and-take and be present for your own speaking and playing. Breathe and listen mindfully, if it helps you stay present and connected.

- If your attention wanders or judgments arise, kindly notice what's happened and bring your attention back to your pet.

- Allow yourself to receive the gifts of love, companionship, and belonging.

97 FREE FROM IT ALL

Many of us are in the position of caring for elderly family members. Caretakers experience excessive stress, which can drain your energy reserves for other loved ones who need you too. The following exercise will help to relieve your stored-up mental strain and refuel you for the journey to be more loving:

- Begin with simple stretching movements for igniting the blood flow and releasing tension. Place both arms over your head and reach for the sky, and then gently drop your arms and bend your body to hang over your toes. Try this a few times.

- Now take a minute to check in with yourself. Are you exhausted and depleted? Overwhelmed and feeling under attack? Anxious and spread too thin?

- Give yourself permission to let it all go. For five whole minutes, if you can, you are not responsible for anything or anyone.

- Say aloud your affirmation: "In this moment, I am not in control of every detail. I am taking care of just myself right now so that I can return with more affection and better attention for others."

98 NEVER ALONE

In your next mindful breath, or through your next mindful moment, the world might reach out its hand to you. You need never feel alone if you can receive the unfolding gift of life. This practice will help you develop a sense of how you're an integral part of the whole of the universe.

Breathe or listen mindfully for about a minute.

- Set your intention. For example, "May this practice deepen my sense of belonging and connection."

- Shift your attention to sounds.

- Open yourself to and receive all sounds directly and mindfully. Focus on each sound's vibration, not names or stories you attach to the sounds. Include the space between sounds.

- Imagine that the vibrations are reaching out to comfort you. Imagine that the universe itself is reaching out—kindly—to you, in the totality of its richness and wholeness through each sound vibration.

- Enjoy the variety—loud, soft, harsh, peaceful, urgent, steady, happy, whatever. Feel the vibration. Let this deep vibration and interconnection with the universe enliven your heart, mind, and body.

- Recognize how the universal energies are always flowing in and through you. You cannot fall out of the universe.

99 OPEN TO THE MYSTERY OF BEING HUMAN

So much of the misery and pain of human life rests upon feelings of fear, separation, and judgment.

This practice invites you to explore some other human possibilities—through meditative reflection, imagination, and inner wisdom.

- Breathe mindfully for about a minute.

- Set your intention. For example, "May this practice awaken me to more possibility."

- Breathe mindfully for a few more breaths.

- Ask yourself the following questions:

  "What would it be like to feel more love in my life?"

  "What if I didn't have to always be right?"

  "What would it feel like to be flowing with life, not against it?"

  "What would it be like to love another more generously?"

After each question, breathe mindfully and listen for whatever answer arises. Work with one question, more than one, or make up your own.

End by opening your eyes and moving gently.

Jeffrey Brantley, MD, is professor emeritus in the department of psychiatry and human behavior at Duke University Medical Center. He is founder and former director of the Mindfulness-Based Stress Reduction (MBSR) Program at Duke Integrative Medicine. He has represented the Duke MBSR program in numerous radio, television, and print interviews. He is author of *Calming Your Anxious Mind*, and coauthor of the *Five Good Minutes®* series.

Wendy Millstine is a freelance writer and certified holistic nutrition consultant who specializes in diet and stress reduction. With Jeffrey Brantley, she is coauthor of the *Five Good Minutes®* series, *Daily Meditations for Calming Your Anxious Mind*, *Daily Meditations for Calming Your Angry Mind*, and *True Belonging*. Millstine is also coauthor of *Calming the Rush of Panic*. She lives in Santa Rosa, CA.

MORE BOOKS from
NEW HARBINGER PUBLICATIONS

JUST ONE THING
Developing a Buddha Brain
One Simple Practice at a Time

978-1608820313 / US $17.95

THE LITTLE BOOK
OF BIG CHANGE
The No-Willpower Approach
to Breaking Any Habit

978-1626252301 / US $16.95

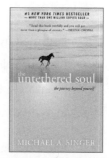

THE UNTETHERED SOUL
The Journey Beyond Yourself

978-1572245372 / US $18.95

THE MIND-BODY
STRESS RESET
Somatic Practices to
Reduce Overwhelm and
Increase Well-Being

978-1684034277 / US $17.95

THE INTUITIVE
EATING JOURNAL
Your Guided Journey for
Nourishing a Healthy
Relationship with Food

978-1684037087 / US $16.95

A HAPPIER YOU
A Seven-Week Program to
Transform Negative Thinking
into Positivity and Resilience

978-1684037858 / US $18.95

ABOUT US

Founded by psychologist Matthew McKay and Patrick
Fanning, New Harbinger has published books that
promote wellness in mind, body, and spirit for more than
forty-five years.

Our proven-effective self-help books and pioneering
workbooks help readers of all ages and backgrounds
make positive lifestyle changes, improve mental health
and well-being, and achieve meaningful personal growth.
In addition, our spirituality books offer profound
guidance for deepening awareness and cultivating
healing, self-discovery, and fulfillment.

New Harbinger is proud to be an independent and
employee-owned company, publishing books that reflect
its core values of integrity, innovation, commitment,
sustainability, compassion, and trust. Written by leaders
in the field and recommended by therapists worldwide,
New Harbinger books are practical, reliable, and provide
real tools for real change.